V-22 OSPREYS

BY CARLOS ALVAREZ

Are you ready to take it to the extreme?
Torque books thrust you into the action-packed
world of sports, vehicles, and adventure. These books
may include dirt, smoke, fire, and dangerous stunts.
WARNING: read at your own risk.

Library of Congress Cataloging-in-Publication Data

Alvarez, Carlos, 1968-
 V-22 Ospreys / by Carlos Alvarez.
    p. cm. – (Torque: military machines)
 Summary: "Amazing photography accompanies engaging information about V-22 Ospreys. The
combination of high-interest subject matter and light text is intended for students in grades 3 through
7"–Provided by publisher.
 Includes bibliographical references and index.
 ISBN 978-1-60014-333-5 (hardcover : alk. paper)
 1. V-22 Osprey (Transport plane)–Juvenile literature. 2. Transport planes–United States–Juvenile
literature. 3. Aeronautics, Military–United States. I. Title.
 UG1242.T7A48 2010
 623.74'65–dc22

                                    2009037751

The images in this book are reproduced through the courtesy of: Ted Carlson / Fotodynamics, p. 7, (top),
p. 20 (top); all other photos courtesy of the   Department of Defense.

Printed in the United States of America, North Mankato, MN.
010110   1149

CONTENTS

THE V-22 OSPREY IN ACTION

Two spinning **rotors** hum as a V-22 Osprey takes off. The aircraft rises into the air like a helicopter. Its rotors tilt forward and the Osprey speeds off like an airplane.

The Osprey carries 24 United States Marines. The crew's **mission** is to drop the Marines behind enemy lines. The aircraft reaches its destination. It lands and the Marines jump to the ground. Then the Osprey rises high into the air and heads back to base. Its mission is complete.

★ FAST FACT ★

The Osprey can also serve as a search-and-rescue aircraft. Crews use it to find and rescue people lost at sea.

VERTICAL TAKE-OFF AND LANDING AIRCRAFT

The V-22 Osprey is a cross between an airplane and a helicopter. It can take off and land like a helicopter. This ability is called **vertical take-off and landing (VTOL)**. The Osprey can **hover** in one place. The Osprey can also tilt its rotors forward so that it travels like an airplane.

The Osprey can fly twice as fast as a military helicopter. It can go five times as far. It can carry three times as

The U.S. military began plans for the Osprey in 1980. The new aircraft was a joint-service project. All the branches of the U.S. military worked together to design it. The Osprey passed flight tests in 2005.

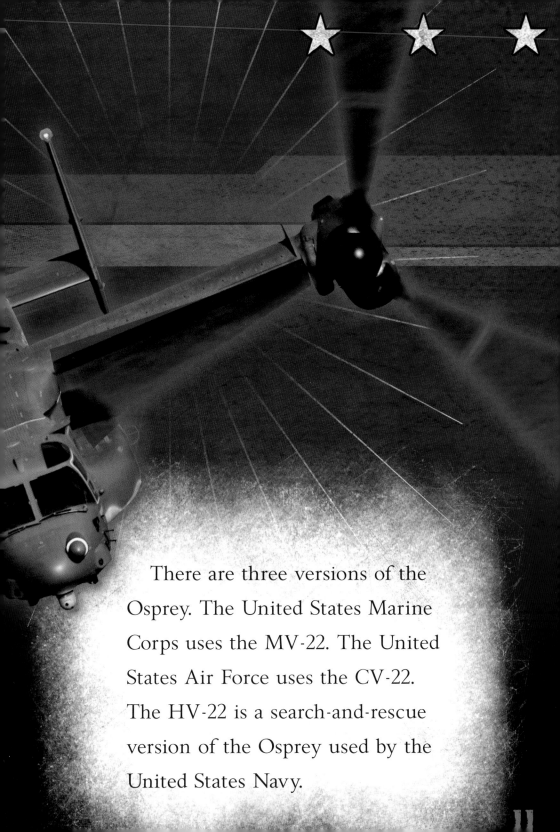

There are three versions of the Osprey. The United States Marine Corps uses the MV-22. The United States Air Force uses the CV-22. The HV-22 is a search-and-rescue version of the Osprey used by the United States Navy.

WEAPONS AND FEATURES

The Osprey's main feature is its tilting rotor system. The aircraft works like a helicopter when the rotors and engines are in the vertical position. The rotors and engines can tilt forward once the aircraft is in the air. This turns the Osprey into a **turboprop aircraft**. The Osprey can then fly faster, farther, and higher than a helicopter.

13

The Osprey has two rotors.
It has one on each side of its body.
The rotors spin in opposite directions.
This feature allows the aircraft to fly
without a tail rotor.

An Osprey crew uses sensors and weapons to complete missions. Advanced **radar** and other sensors help detect threats and targets. The Osprey is not heavily armed. It has one M240 **machine gun**. This 7.62mm gun can shoot more than 500 bullets per minute.

V-22 OSPREY SPECIFICATIONS:

Primary Function: Vertical take-off and landing (VTOL) aircraft

Length: 57 feet, 4 inches (17.4 meters)

Height: 22 feet, 1 inch (6.7 meters)

Wingspan: 84 feet, 7 inches (25.8 meters)

Rotor Diameter: 38 feet (11.6 meters)

Maximum VTOL Weight: 52,870 pounds (23,980 kilograms)

Top Speed: 277 miles (446 kilometers) per hour

Ceiling: 25,000 feet (7,600 meters)

Engines: Two Rolls Royce AE1107C turboshaft engines

Crew: Up to 4

V-22 MISSIONS

The Osprey's main mission is to carry combat troops into battle. It can carry 24 troops. **Special forces** use the Osprey to get behind enemy lines. The Osprey must quickly move in and out of enemy territory. It does not want to be spotted.

The Osprey is named for a bird of prey. The osprey is a bird that eats fish. It is also known as a sea hawk.

The Osprey can have a crew of up to four. The pilot and co-pilot fly the Osprey. Two flight engineers control radar, communications gear, and weapons. The Osprey's many features help the crew complete dangerous missions.

GLOSSARY

hover—to hang in the air without forward or backward movement

machine gun—an automatic weapon that rapidly fires bullets

mission—a military task

radar—a sensor system that uses radio waves to locate objects in the air

rotor—a set of rotating blades that gives a helicopter its lift

special forces—troops trained in several kinds of warfare

turboprop aircraft—an aircraft that gets its thrust from sets of spinning blades

vertical take-off and landing (VTOL)—the ability to take off and land without the need for a runway

TO LEARN MORE

AT THE LIBRARY

Alvarez, Carlos. *Marine Expeditionary Units.* Minneapolis, Minn.: Bellwether Media, 2010.

David, Jack. *United States Marine Corps.* Minneapolis, Minn.: Bellwether Media, 2008.

Hopkins, Ellen. *U.S. Air Force Fighting Vehicles.* Chicago, Ill.: Heinemann Library, 2004.

ON THE WEB

Learning more about military machines is as easy as 1, 2, 3.

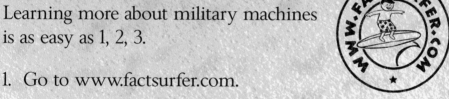

1. Go to www.factsurfer.com.

2. Enter "military machines" into the search box.

3. Click the "Surf" button and you will see a list of related Web sites.

With factsurfer.com, finding more information is just a click away.

INDEX